MORE ALL-AGE TALKS
FOR
Lent,
HOLY WEEK
& EASTER

NICK FAWCETT

kevin mayhew

kevin
mayhew

First published in Great Britain in 2015 by Kevin Mayhew Ltd
Buxhall, Stowmarket, Suffolk IP14 3BW
Tel: +44 (0) 1449 737978 Fax: +44 (0) 1449 737834
E-mail: info@kevinmayhew.com

www.kevinmayhew.com

9 8 7 6 5 4 3 2 1 0

ISBN 978 1 84867 784 5
Catalogue No. 1501480

Cover design by Rob Mortonson
© Images used under licence from Shutterstock Inc.
Illustrations by Steve English
Typeset by Angela Selfe

Printed and bound in Great Britain

Contents

About the author

Brought up in Southend-in-Sea, Essex, Nick Fawcett trained for the Baptist ministry at Bristol and Oxford, before serving churches in Lancashire and Cheltenham. He subsequently spent three years as a chaplain with the Christian movement Toc H, before focusing on writing and editing, which he continues with today, despite wrestling with myeloma, a currently incurable cancer of the bone marrow. He lives with his wife, Deborah, and two children – Samuel and Kate – in Wellington, Somerset, worshipping, when able, at the local Anglican church. A keen walker, he delights in the beauty of the Somerset and Devon countryside around his home, his numerous books owing much to the inspiration he unfailingly finds there.

Nick has had over 130 books published by Kevin Mayhew. For further details, please refer to our website: www.kevinmayhew.com

Introduction

I will never forget the day at Bristol College when I received the orders of service prior to my first preaching engagement and saw leaping out at me two words: Children's Talk. Clearly this was viewed as an integral part of the service, but what exactly was expected of me, still less how I could deliver it, I had no idea. My experience in talking to children was, to say the least, limited, and there was little I had learned up to that point which had prepared me for the task. Had I but known it, no formal training was to be offered in this field anyway, the learning process essentially consisting of being thrown in at the deep end.

I squirm with embarrassment when I look back on some of the early 'children's talks' I delivered, the content simplistic if not down-right patronising. Numerous congregations must have exercised enormous patience as slowly I developed my technique at their expense. Yet, strangely, the person who taught me more about the art of successful communication than anyone else was not a member of any single congregation, nor one of my college tutors, but an elocutionist I saw for a few brief sessions during my time at Bristol College. His advice consisted of three simple tips:

- always begin by asking a question or using an illustration that involves your audience in what you are saying;
- always end with a simple challenge or question that puts in a nut-shell everything you have been trying to say;
- keep the middle short, simple and to the point.

In every address I have given since then I have kept that advice in mind, not following it slavishly but attempting to apply the essential principles whenever possible. They have stood me in good stead. While I have never considered myself a particularly gifted preacher, still less a natural communicator, the talks I have given throughout my ministry seem generally to have been well received. Why? Partly perhaps because my talks were always short, but most of all, I believe, because listeners could always find something to relate to.

Having said that, every talk is different. The style of a sermon is quite unlike that of a lecture – at least it should be! The style of a wedding address is nothing like that of a funeral oration. Similarly, the style of a children's talk – or family talk, as I prefer to call it – is totally different again. When young people are present in church you are immediately talking to a wide age-range, spanning two, three or even four generations. It is essential not to talk down to children, and equally important that adults get something more from the talk than a pleasant sense of indulgence. This is all the more important if my suspicion is correct that many adults actually prefer listening to a family-type talk than a sermon, the latter often being pitched so far over their heads that their thoughts soon wander to such matters as the state of their Sunday lunch or yesterday's football results!

So what makes a successful family talk? There is no one answer to that, but for me the following are all vital ingredients:

- an element of fun
- appropriate visual aids
- 'audience' participation
- all-age relevance
- brief applications
- thorough preparation
- attractive presentation.

Let me deal with each of these in turn.

Fun

With any audience a little light-heartedness goes a long way towards establishing a rapport. When talking to young people this becomes all the more essential, as there are so many other attractions in our society competing for their time. Too often I have attended services in which the 'talk to the children' is little more than a mini (or not so mini) sermon, and the ineffectiveness of this approach has been eloquently testified to by scarcely suppressed expressions of boredom. Not only do such talks fail to get the message across but, far worse, they effectively drive young people away from our churches.

Visual Aids

My own preference has always been to include some sort of visual aid in a talk, even if this is simply key words stuck to a board. Indeed, words and words games, as you will see, figure prominently throughout this book. It is a fact that what we see stays in our minds far longer than what we simply hear.

Audience Participation

Young people (and many older ones too) like to be involved in a 'learning process' rather than simply being talked to. Games, word-searches, quizzes and other such forms of participation offer an effective way of including the congregation in what you are saying. We need to promote an atmosphere in which people feel part of what is going on.

All-age Relevance

As I have said already, many adults are actually far more receptive to a talk geared towards a younger audience than they are to a sermon. Many also enjoy participation as much as children, if not more so! Even if this were not the case, we owe it to any congregation to ensure that a talk is able both to stimulate and challenge.

Brief Applications

I have always believed that the secret of a successful family talk is to keep the application – the serious bit at the end – as short and simple as possible. Ideally, the message you are looking to put across (and this ought to be one message, not several) should speak for itself through the illustrations and visual aids you use, though some expansion of what this means is usually necessary. Overdo the application and you will pay the price. Which of us hasn't witnessed the sudden glazed looks the moment the 'religious' part of a talk is reached. Whatever you do, don't try and ram the point home; if you haven't made the point through the fun part of your talk, you won't make it afterwards.

Thorough Preparation

There is no getting away from it: talking to young people takes time. There were many occasions during my ministry when I spent longer preparing a single family talk (even one lasting a mere five minutes) than two full-length sermons. In this book I have attempted to do most of the spadework for you through suggesting ideas and ways of presenting these, but to deliver most of the talks you will still need to spend some time in preparation. Don't be put off by this. The effort may occasionally seem out of proportion to the time taken up by the talk during the service, but I believe the results will more than justify it. What you put in, you will get out.

Attractive Presentation

In this sophisticated age, young people as much as adults are used to slick, glossy and professional presentations. While we cannot emulate these, it is important for visual material to be as clear and well presented as possible. Home computers and modern technology make this far easier to achieve than it once was, as well as saving huge amounts of time. While material can be written out by hand (for many of these talks I did just that), I would strongly recommend the use of a PC word-processing package if possible. When it comes to displaying material, my own preference, arrived at after several years of trial and error, was to use a magnetic whiteboard in conjunction with magnetic tape (available through most office stationery suppliers), with the back-up of a second whiteboard (magnetic or otherwise) and sticky tack. If you choose this method, you will need easels for these, as light and portable as possible. A supply of thick coloured marker pens (in washable and permanent ink) is a must for many talks, as is a copious supply of thin card and/or paper. Many of the talks nowadays could be delivered using an overhead projector and screen if this is preferred to board and easel. Adapt to your available resources. On a purely practical note, make use of a radio microphone if this is available. Family talks often involve a degree of movement, and it is all too easy to stray from a standing microphone so that you become inaudible, or, worse still, to trip headlong over the wires of a halterneck model! (The younger members of the congregation will delight in this, but for you it can prove embarrassing and even dangerous.) Each talk in this collection is set out according to a basic framework:

- a suggested Bible passage which should normally be read publicly prior to the talk
- a statement of the aim of the talk
- details of preparation needed beforehand
- the talk itself.

This last section includes instructions relating, for example, to the use of illustrations, together with a suggested application of the talk. The talks will work best if, having read and digested these paragraphs, you present them in your own words. This is particularly true where the congregation is invited to respond, and developing and incorporating their ideas and answers into the talk will require a measure of ad-libbing on your part.

Each of the talks in this booklet was used in public worship during my time in the ministry. No doubt many are flawed in places and could be considerably improved – I do not offer them as examples of how it should be done, but rather as a resource which may be of help to you. Of all the comments received during my ministry, few have gratified me more than those when young people have referred in conversation to talks I delivered three, four, even five years back. Whether they remembered the point I had been making I cannot say, but, whatever else, they clearly enjoyed being in church and carried away positive associations of their time there. That in itself was always sufficient motivation to spend further time and energy devoted to getting the message across.

Nick Fawcett

LENT

Don't Waste It

Reading Luke 12:42-48

Aim This talk, designed for Shrove Tuesday (so, strictly speaking, outside of Lent), picks up and enlarges on the significance of making pancakes, asking what lessons this tradition might have for us today.

Preparation Make three pancake shapes out of modelling clay, Plasticene or playdough, and then, using more modelling clay of another colour, mould some letters to spell out RESOURCES, GIFTS and LENT. Press these down (making one word for each) into the 'pancakes'. Place the two 'pancakes' labelled GIFTS and LENT into a large mixing bowl and the one labelled RESOURCES into a frying pan, word facing downwards. Position the mixing bowl and frying pan on a table at the front of the church. Conceal a box of eggs, a pint of milk, a bag of flour, a container of salt and a pat of butter somewhere around the church.

Talk Depending on the time/day of the service/talk, ask how many people had or will be having pancakes today/this week. Ask if anyone can tell you why pancakes are traditionally eaten on Shrove Tuesday. Explain that pancake-making is a particularly English tradition, originally started to use up stocks of fat, butter and eggs, which, along with meat (not used in pancakes!), were all foods forbidden during the period of Lent, when Christians traditionally fasted to mark the 40 days Jesus fasted in the wilderness before facing temptation. These food items would not keep for 40 days, but poor people particularly couldn't afford to waste precious provisions, so they used them up in the pancakes, enjoying something of a feast in doing so.

In some places, Pancake Day races are still held, such as in the Buckinghamshire town of Olney, where races have taken place ever since 1445, when, so the story goes, a woman was cooking pancakes and, hearing the church shriving-bell summoning people to confession, rushed to church in her apron, still clutching hold of her frying pan.

Ask if anyone can find the ingredients of pancakes that you have hidden around the church. As they are brought forward to you, explain their meaning:

- eggs – symbol of creation
- milk – symbol of purity
- flour – the staff of life
- salt – symbol of wholesomeness
- butter – used as a fat to cook the mixture in.

Tell the congregation that you want to focus particularly on the idea behind pancakes of avoiding waste. Place these 'ingredients' (still in their containers) into the mixing bowl on your table; as you do so, place the modelling-clay pancakes labelled GIFTS and LENT on top. Tell the congregation that you are going to make three special pancakes for them, and that you will need three volunteers to toss them for you. Give your first volunteer the frying pan to hold, and ask him or her to toss the 'pancake' inside it. Afterwards, hold this up, revealing the word RESOURCES. Of all the things we cannot afford to waste, resources are perhaps those most often in the news today. We are increasingly coming to realise that supplies of commodities like fuel, minerals, timber and much else are limited and therefore need to be used thoughtfully and wisely, and recycled where possible. As Christians, we have a responsibility to be at the forefront in stewarding this world's resources.

Take the 'pancake' marked GIFTS, place it in the frying pan, and ask a second volunteer to toss it, once again displaying the word on the pancake afterwards. If there's a danger of wasting resources on a global scale, there's equally a danger on an individual level – namely, wasting our gifts. We may be gifted in science or languages, maths or literature, music or graphic design, or perhaps in sport, carpentry or metalwork. Do we make the most of such gifts, developing them to their full potential? Equally, there are gifts in a wider sense: things like health and education. Again, do we make the most of what God has given us?

Ask a third volunteer to toss your final 'pancake', this time revealing the word LENT. Not as many Christians fast today during Lent as was once the case, but many still observe the season in some way. Some make time for prayer or quiet reflection, some meet with Christians of other denominations in study groups, some attempt to kick a bad habit, while others deny themselves certain 'luxuries', giving the money they would have spent to charity or other good causes. Lent marks out 40 days distinct from the rest of the year – once again, we should not waste it.

The simple pancake, as well as providing a tasty meal, has much to teach us. Its lesson is summed up in the last verse of our reading:

> 'From everyone to whom much has been given, much will be required; and from one to whom much has been entrusted, even more will be demanded' (Luke 12:48).

Whatever God gives you, don't waste it.

Choosing the Way

Reading   Matthew 3:13-4:22; ensure this is read BEFORE the talk.

Aim   To emphasise the importance of choices in life and to explore what might help us in coming to the right decisions.

Preparation   This talk is based on the old TV programme *Blockbusters*. It requires a considerable amount of work, but the enjoyment it gives makes the effort well worth it.

You will need to prepare a grid of hexagons similar to the one below, and to write a different letter of the alphabet in each of the hexagons. I have not used the letters 'x' or 'y', so no questions are provided for these letters. *Blockbusters* used a smaller grid, but this larger size offers scope for more questions.

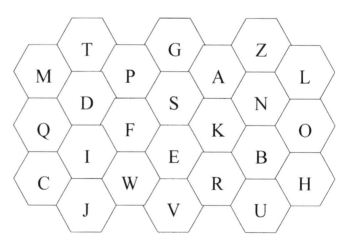

The lettered grid can be prepared in various ways. You might wish to mark it directly on to a whiteboard, you could draw it on a large sheet of card or paper, or you could prepare it on an acetate sheet or computer ready for overhead projection. Alternatively, you could cut out individual hexagons (24 in all) and fix these to a whiteboard using sticky tack. This takes more time but has the advantage of allowing you to reconfigure the board for a second game. Whichever way you choose, you will need to have some way of highlighting hexagons once a correct answer has been given. Unless you are using some kind of projection method, cut out individual hexagons using pieces of blue and pink card (a different colour for each team/participant). When someone answers correctly, cover the lettered hexagon with the appropriate coloured hexagon. If using the projection method, you will need to shade the hexagon with a piece of coloured acetate, or use 'fill' on a computer.

The original *Blockbusters* is a game for two individuals, but I recommend dividing the congregation into two teams. This is more likely to hold the attention of all and allows everyone the chance to participate. Always ensure, however, that younger people have the chance to answer before older folk leap in.

Talk Divide the congregation into roughly two halves, telling them that you have devised a game along the lines of the television programme *Blockbusters*. Display the grid you have prepared and explain that the aim of the game is, through correctly answering questions related to today's Bible reading, to turn letters to the colour of your team in a continuous sequence from the top to the bottom of the grid.

The first person to put their hand up (it may be worth enlisting the help of someone to spot each time who this is) will get to answer the question. If a wrong answer is given, the other team have ten seconds to come up with the right one. The answer in each case begins with the letter chosen. Should no correct answer be given, another question beginning with the same letter is asked. When a team answers correctly, it has the choice of the next letter.

Select the blue team to start, and ask them to choose the first letter.

A list of questions for each letter of the alphabet is given below (cross out the questions as you go along, to make sure you don't ask the same one twice!). It may be worth having a list of emergency questions, just in case you have need of them.

A

Which 'A' did the Scriptures say would protect Jesus if he jumped off the temple? (ANGELS)

Which 'A' was John the Baptist placed under? (ARREST)

B

Which 'B' did Jesus go through before he went into the wilderness? (BAPTISM)

Which 'B' was Jesus tempted to turn stones into? (BREAD)

C

At which 'C' was Jesus crucified? (CALVARY)

Which 'C' did the way Jesus chose finally lead to? (CROSS)

D

Which 'D' descended on Jesus after his baptism? (DOVE)

Which 'D' tempted Jesus? (DEVIL)

E

Which 'E', meaning the opposite of hard, describes the way Jesus refused to take? (EASY)

Which 'E', the opposite of good, is involved in temptation? (EVIL)

F

Which 'F' is the number of days Jesus spent in the desert? (FORTY)

Which 'F' means to go without food? (FAST)

G

Which place beginning with 'G' was the scene of much of Jesus' ministry both before and after his temptation? (GALILEE)

Which 'G' means the place of the skull? (GOLGOTHA)

H

Which 'H' describes how Jesus felt about 40 days without food? (HUNGER)

Which 'H' was the name of the 'kings' ruling in Judah when Jesus was born and when he was crucified? (HEROD)

I

Which 'I' is the country in which the ministry of Jesus took place? (ISRAEL)

Which 'I's words did Jesus fulfil by going to Capernaum? (ISAIAH)

J

Which 'J' was Jesus baptised in? (JORDAN)

In which 'J' was the temple? (JERUSALEM)

K

Which 'K's did the devil promise Jesus if he would bow down to him? (KINGDOMS)

Which 'K' describes what the devil ask Jesus to do? (KNEEL)

L

Which 'L' is a season recalling the temptation of Jesus? (LENT)

Which 'L' did Jesus bring to those living in darkness? (LIGHT)

M

Which 'M' describes what James and John were doing to their nets when Jesus called them? (MENDING)

Which 'M' did the devil lead Jesus on to? (MOUNTAINTOP)

N

Which 'N' didn't Jesus return to after his temptation? (NAZARETH)

In which 'N' was Capernaum? (NAPHTALI)

O

Which 'O' describes what happened to the heavens after Jesus' baptism? (OPENED)

Which 'O', meaning doing as we are told, did Jesus show in relation to God? (OBEDIENCE)

P

Which 'P' condemned Jesus to be crucified? (PONTIUS PILATE)

Which 'P' did Jesus call to be a disciple? (PETER)

Q

Which 'Q's are we asked during any time of examination? (QUESTIONS)

Which 'Q' means to say what someone else has written? (QUOTE)

R

Which 'R' did John the Baptist call the people to? (REPENTANCE)

Which 'R', the opposite of wrong, was Jesus determined to do? (RIGHT)

S

Which 'S' led Jesus out into the wilderness? (SPIRIT)

Which 'S' was Jesus tempted to turn into bread? (STONES)

T

Which 'T' describes what Jesus faced in the wilderness? (TEMPTATION)

Which 'T' was Jesus tempted to throw himself off? (TEMPLE)

U

Which feeling of 'U' did John the Baptist feel when Jesus asked to be baptised? (UNWORTHINESS)

Which 'U' describes the fire that John the Baptist spoke of? (UNQUENCHABLE)

V

Which 'V' came from heaven after Jesus was baptised? (VOICE)

John called the Pharisees and Sadducees a 'brood of' which 'V'? (VIPERS)

W

Which 'W' was Jesus led into to be tempted? (WILDERNESS)

Which 'W' did the devil want Jesus to kneel and offer to him? (WORSHIP)

Z

Which 'Z' was a land on the other side of the Jordan? (ZEBULUN)

Which 'Z' was the father of James and John? (ZEBEDEE)

Play another game after the first has finished, provided you have enough questions left for a second round. This time, allow the pink team first choice of colour.

The aim of the game is very simple: to make the right choices and then find the right answers that will see you safely through. In each game you have to decide on the best path to take, just as Jesus had to decide out in the wilderness during the time of his temptation. There, at the beginning of his ministry, he had to make choices that would have far-reaching consequences. He had to decide on the right way forward, the path God had chosen for him: whether to live for himself, or live and die for others; whether to seek an earthly kingdom and worldly glory, or to work for God's eternal kingdom, bringing it closer here on earth. The way he chose, of course, was God's way. For us, too, life is full of choices, some of them easy and some difficult. On occasions the right way forward is clear; at other times we must take a step of faith, trusting that we are doing the right thing. The temptation of Jesus, however, offers us guidelines in making those choices. Will we serve our own interests only or consider the needs of others as well? Will we take the way of least resistance or take the path that we know to be right even if it proves costly? Will we follow the way of the world or ask God for guidance, asking what he is saying to us? Will we give in to temptation or resist that which we know to be wrong? Lent reminds us of the need to choose throughout our lives. Which will we follow: our way or God's way?

You Decide

Readings   Matthew 12:33-37; 1 John 1:5-10

Aim   This talk, like the last, focuses on the importance of choices, but we focus here more on the idea of being responsible for our own decisions and actions. Though God offers guidance, whether or not we follow him is finally down to us.

Preparation   No special preparation is needed for this talk.

Talk   Tell the congregation that you are going to play a simple Question of Sport game. (You may wish to divide people into two teams, to introduce a fun competitive element to the talk.) All the questions are concerned with sporting officials and the decisions they might take.

- In what sport might a penalty be awarded for handball? *(Football)*
- What name do we give to the person who makes that decision? *(Referee)*
- In what game might someone be given out stumped/caught behind? *(Cricket)*
- Who makes that decision? *(Umpire)*
- In what sport might a try be awarded? *(Rugby)*
- Who makes that decision? *(Referee)*
- In what sport might the winner squeeze home by a short head? *(Horse-racing)*
- Who makes that decision? *(Steward)*
- In what sport might a false start be called? *(Athletics: track events)*
- Who would make such a call? *(Starter)*
- In what sport might someone call 'touching ball'? *(Snooker)*
- Who makes that decision? *(Referee)*
- In what sport might a points' decision be needed to decide the outcome? *(Boxing)*
- Who makes such a decision? *(Judges)*

These are just a few of the sports people play and the decisions taken within them. In each case a particular official is entrusted with the responsibility of deciding between right and wrong, between what's allowed and what isn't. But let's have a couple more questions:

- In which sport might someone say a club has been grounded in the sand or a wrong ball been played? *(Golf)*
- Who makes that decision? *(The player concerned)*

In golf, as in other sports, there are officials on the course and a tournament referee, but part of the etiquette of the game is that each player acknowledges when they have infringed the rules. There's no arguing with the referee or disputing decisions; if players do something wrong, even inadvertently, they hold their hands up and shoulder the responsibility (as is also true in snooker).

There are parallels in all this with daily life. Sometimes rules are imposed upon us, whether at school or work or simply as citizens bound by the law of this country, and when we break those rules there is someone to reprimand and impose a penalty on us. But there are also times when we must decide for ourselves between right and wrong, and when we must have the courage to admit our mistakes. The time will come, says Jesus, when we are called to account, but it is up to us to decide here and now how we act. No one will force us to take his way, no one will know many of the things we do or think; no one, that is, but us. Are we ready to acknowledge our faults? Do we have the honesty to face up to where we go wrong? No one else can do that for us; *we* must decide.

Turning Around

Readings   Mark 1:1-8; 2 Corinthians 5:16-21

Aim   To emphasise that being a Christian involves a constant turning around from our old way of life to new life in Christ.

Preparation   Using large letters on a whiteboard or OHP, print the following down the left-hand side of the board/acetate:

> LOOT
>
> EVIL
>
> MOOR
>
> DRAWER
>
> FLOG
>
> LEER
>
> REMIT
>
> POOL
>
> TRAP
>
> LIAR
>
> STOP
>
> SNOOPS
>
> STRESSED
>
> REVEL
>
> TRAMS

On separate strips of card/paper, print the words below, attach a piece of sticky tack, and retain these for use during the talk (if you are using an OHP, you will need to write these on to the acetate during the course of the talk):

> TOOL, LIVE, ROOM, REWARD, GOLF, REEL, TIMER, LOOP, PART, RAIL, POTS, SPOONS, DESSERTS, LEVER, SMART

Talk Show the congregation the list of words and ask how many words they can see there? The obvious answer, of course, is 15. Explain that although this is right in one sense, in another sense it is wrong, for these words all have something special about them. Ask if anyone can spot what it is. The answer is that each word can be read backwards as well as forwards. Run through the list, asking if anyone can identify the words reading backwards.

LOOT	TOOL
EVIL	LIVE
MOOR	ROOM
DRAWER	REWARD
FLOG	GOLF
LEER	REEL
REMIT	TIMER
POOL	LOOP
TRAP	PART
LIAR	RAIL
STOP	POTS
SNOOPS	SPOONS
STRESSED	DESSERTS
REVEL	LEVER
TRAMS	SMART

It isn't just words that can be turned round to become something else; today's readings remind us that people can also have their lives turned around in such a way that we can speak of them becoming a different person. That is what John the Baptist was saying as he preached in the wilderness proclaiming the coming of Jesus, and that is what God in Christ has made possible for you, for me and for everyone:

> If anyone is in Christ, there is a new creation: everything old has passed away; see, everything has become new! (2 Corinthians 5:17)

Whatever we are, whoever we are, God is always able, through his love, to turn our lives round and make them something completely different, but to do so he needs our willingness to change direction, to follow a new course, to turn each day from the old to the new. Do that, and like these words here, our lives will take on new meaning.

Whose Side Are You On?

Readings   Joshua 24:14-28; Colossians 2:6-7

Aim   To emphasise the need for a lasting commitment rather than temporary allegiance to Christ.

Preparation   Given the ever-changing world of football, you may need to update this talk to allow for recent developments in the transfer market. Check that players are still with the clubs indicated and, if necessary, add your own to the list.

Talk   Ask how many people like football. Apologise to those who don't and explain that you have a quiz today about football players and the teams they play for. Ask which sides the following are part of:

- Wayne Rooney   *Manchester United*
- Aaron Ramsey   *Arsenal*
- Daniel Sturridge   *Liverpool*
- Sergio Agüero   *Manchester City*
- Fraser Forster   *Southampton*
- Stewart Downing   *West Ham United*
- Harry Kane   *Tottenham Hotspur*
- Eden Hazard   *Chelsea*
- Leighton Baines   *Everton*

Football fans will have had no problem in identifying which teams these play for, but they will also know that in a season's time it might well be different. Players are often involved with several clubs during the course of their career. They may give their all each time, but with every change of club their loyalties are suddenly switched.

Take the following: what team do the following play for now and what team did they join that club from?

- Wilfried Bony

  Now Manchester City, formerly Swansea

- Juan Mata

  Now Manchester United, formerly Chelsea

- Adam Lallana

  Now Liverpool, formerly Southampton

- Danny Welbeck

  Now Arsenal, formerly Manchester United

- Jake Livermore

  Now Hull City, formerly Spurs

- Romelu Lukaku

  Now Everton, formerly Chelsea

In football, as in many areas of life, there's nothing wrong with changing direction – for many players it is part of a gradual progression to the top – but in some things, such as family relationships and when it comes to serving God, it's essential. That's the message Joshua was emphasising to the people of Israel in our reading:

> If you would rather not serve the Lord, then choose this day whom you will serve, whether the gods your ancestors served in the region beyond the Euphrates or the gods of the Amorites in whose land you are living; but as for me and my household, we will serve the Lord. (Joshua 24:15, own translation)

And that's the message Paul was similarly driving home in his letter to the Colossians:

> As you therefore have received Christ Jesus the Lord, continue to live your lives in him, rooted and built up in him and established in the faith, just as you were taught, abounding in thanksgiving. (Colossians 2:6-7, own translation)

'Whose side are you on?' says Joshua. 'Keep faithful,' says Paul. Commitment to Christ isn't a five-minute wonder, something we can toy with for a while before moving on to something else. It's about a lifetime's loyalty, staying true through thick and thin, continuing in the faith to the end. Whose side are we on today? More important, whose side will we be on tomorrow, the next day and the next day?

Recognising our Mistakes

Readings   1 John 1:5-10; 2 Samuel 12:1-7 (NIV version. Have someone read this immediately before the talk, and urge the congregation to listen especially carefully in readiness for what will follow.)

Aim   To bring home the importance of recognising and acknowledging our mistakes if we are to enjoy a right relationship with God.

Preparation   No special preparation is needed for this talk.

Talk   Ask the congregation how good they are at spotting mistakes. Tell them that you are going to read the first three verses of the reading from 2 Samuel again and ask them to listen very carefully to make sure you get nothing wrong. Read the 'passage' below, keeping as straight a face as possible.

> The BOARD sent TARZAN to JANE. When he came to TIM, he BLED, 'There were two HENS in a certain GOWN, one A FISH and the other A DOOR. The FISH man had a very large number of SHEETS and RATTLES, but the DOOR man had nothing except one little STEWED RAM he had CAUGHT. He BRAISED it, and it FLEW up with him and his PILGRIM. It SHAVED his WOOD, SHRANK from his PUP, and even CREPT in his FARMS. It was like a SAUCER to him.

Ask if anyone spotted something wrong, and then read the passage again, asking people to put their hands up the moment they spot a mistake and to tell you what the correct word should be. The corrected version in full is as follows:

> The LORD sent NATHAN to DAVID. When he came to HIM, he SAID, 'There were two MEN in a certain TOWN, one RICH and the other POOR. The RICH man had a very large number of

SHEEP and CATTLE, but the POOR man had nothing except one little EWE LAMB he had BOUGHT. He RAISED it, and it GREW up with him and his CHILDREN. It SHARED his FOOD, DRANK from his CUP, and even SLEPT in his ARMS. It was like a DAUGHTER to him.

These words are part of a parable told by the prophet Nathan aimed at forcing King David to confront the truth and to admit his wrong-doing. He had stolen the wife of Uriah, sending Uriah to his death in order to do so, and until he faced up to that fact, his relationship with God would be forever damaged, a mockery of what it should be. The parable, and subsequent events, had the desired effect, David confessing his sin and seeking God's forgiveness.

The first version was, of course, full of mistakes from start to finish, some of them big, some of them small, but all of them were important for they changed the whole meaning of the reading. Those mistakes were put in deliberately, but when it comes to everyday life there are mistakes that we all make without even being aware of them and that stop us from being the people God wants us to be. Lent is a time for looking honestly at our lives and recognising where we have gone wrong; a time for acknowledging our faults and facing up to our mistakes. Have we the courage to do that?

A Tempting Prospect

Readings   Luke 4:1-13; Hebrews 4:14-16

Aim   To illustrate the fact that temptation is very real, coming in all shapes and sizes, but that God, in Christ, is able to help us withstand it.

Preparation   Copy and enlarge the following drawings on to A4-size pieces of paper or card, and stick them in prominent positions around the church. Larger versions of these pictures may be found on pages 35-36.

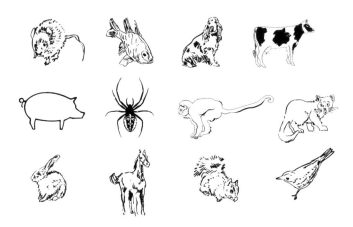

On separate strips of paper / card, print the following in large bold letters and retain for use later in the talk:

BONE, FISH, GRASS, SWILL, MAGGOT, OATS, BANANA, CARROT, NUTS, CHEESE, WORM, FLY

Talk   Our theme today is temptation: what tempts people!
    One by one, stick the words you've printed on to a whiteboard, asking what creature might be tempted by the item in question. Invite whoever gives a correct answer to bring the appropriate picture to you. Fasten this to the board next to the relevant word, as follows:

Bone

Fish

Grass

Swill

Maggot

Oats

Banana

Carrot

Nuts

Cheese

Worm

Fly

Each of these items would be an irresistible temptation to the creatures in question. So how about us? What sort of things would we be tempted by? Part of the answer can be seen in the temptation of Jesus. The temptations he experienced have much in common with those that people still face today: the temptation to gain power, to compromise our convictions, to look after number one at the cost of others, and so on. But, of course, those are only some of the things that tempt us. Money, sex, drugs, alcohol are obvious others, but there are many more, most innocent in themselves but capable of leading us astray if taken out of context or pursued to the exclusion of all else. We will face temptation in a host of different forms, and will all fail on countless occasions, so much so that we will sometimes despair of ever serving Christ as we would want to. Lent, though, is a time that urges us not to give up. It reminds us that Jesus was tempted just as we are, so he understands what we are going through and offers help to fight temptation. It reminds us also that if we fail but are genuinely sorry, seeking forgiveness and strength to try again, he is always ready to show grace and mercy; always prepared to put the past behind us and offer a fresh start.

An Honest Assessment

Reading   Romans 5:8

Aim   To emphasise the importance of Lent as a time to look honestly at who and what we are, and then to acknowledge the good and the bad openly to God, seeking his guidance as to how best to use our strengths and overcome our weaknesses.

Preparation   For this talk you will need a large box with a good-size mirror stuck to the bottom of it, facing upwards. For effect, you might also want to have as a prop an empty medicine bottle labelled 'Smelling salts'.

Talk   Gingerly hold up the box you've prepared, and ask if anyone in the congregation is feeling brave. Double-check that they're really feeling confident, gravely warning that you have something truly horrible to show them, so horrible that you barely dare look yourself! Ask volunteers to come forward, but continue to build up the tension, constantly checking that they want go through with the exercise and offering them the chance to sit down again if they wish. Arrange your volunteers in a group to one side, telling them to keep a safe distance, then ask one to come with you to look into the box. Whisper to them not to let on what they see there. Repeat this with each volunteer, asking him or her afterwards how they feel about what they saw? Was it as horrible as they expected? Was it better? Was it worse?

After the last volunteer has looked inside, tell the congregation that it's time they judged for themselves. Walk round the congregation with the box open (or take out and display the mirror). Observe, light-heartedly, that what each one saw was more horrible than anyone probably expected!

Of course, it wasn't actually horrible at all. But what would you say if I had a mirror that was able to show what's going on inside someone rather than outside, the sort of things we're thinking and feeling? What would we see then, and how pleasant a sight would that be? No doubt there'd be a lot of good things – kind thoughts, fine intentions and so forth – but there would probably also be some not so good things – thoughts, attitudes, intentions that we'd prefer no one to know about.

Thankfully, no one can see what goes on inside our heads – at least no one but God. He sees our best and our worst, our strengths and our weaknesses, the good, the bad and the ugly, and he loves and accepts us as we are – this surely is the most important truth at the heart of Lent. Yet that doesn't mean we should sit back complacently, for God is always looking to help us become the people he knows we can be. He wants us to build on our strengths and to overcome those things that separate us from his love. He wants to nurture what is good and to help us conquer whatever prevents us enjoying living life to the full.

To do that means having the courage to look at ourselves honestly, not at the outside but deep within. It means facing up to our faults, acknowledging where we go wrong, recognising where things are not as they should be, and asking God for help and forgiveness. It means being open to the way God might want to use us and open also to the possibility that we have not been as ready as we might be to use our gifts in his service. Are we ready to take a good hard look at ourselves and see ourselves not as we like to imagine but as we really are?

Spotting the Symptoms

Readings   2 Corinthians 13:5-10; Galatians 5:16-26 (read as part of the talk)

Aim   To bring home the fact that Lent offers a time for us to conduct a thorough self-examination of our spiritual lives, ensuring that our faith is as healthy as it should be.

Preparation   For this talk you can either copy and enlarge (to about A4 size) each picture below or test your own artistic skills! (Larger versions of these pictures may be found on pages 42-43.)

Stick the pictures on to a wall or whiteboard.

On separate slips of card/paper, print the following in large bold letters, ready to display underneath the faces during the talk:

CHICKENPOX, FLU, MUMPS, TOOTHACHE, MEASLES, SCARLET FEVER

Talk   Ask if anyone has had a cold recently and what their symptoms were. Ask if anyone has felt so unwell that they've had to consult a doctor. Point to the faces you have drawn and ask what is wrong with each person.

Chickenpox   Flu   Mumps

Toothache   Measles   Scarlet fever

How can we tell what each is suffering from? What clues give their illnesses away? What other symptoms do we associate with these conditions? (Chickenpox: itching and inflamed spots; Flu: sore throat, streaming eyes, sneezing, blocked up or running nose; Measles: high temperature; etc.)

Sometimes we can spot the symptoms of an illness ourselves; at other times we need to consult an expert to find out what's wrong with us. Either way, when we realise something is wrong, we take action, whether it be going to bed, taking medicine, consulting a dentist, or sipping hot lemon.

Most of us recognise the need to look after our physical health, but we can all too easily forget about our spiritual health. Lent calls us to make time for self-examination, to take a long hard look at ourselves so as to judge what sort of shape we are in spiritually. Is our prayer life what it should be? Are our relationships with God and others right? Are we living in the sort of way that God intends, or giving in to temptation, compromising our convictions? As Paul put it in his second letter to the Corinthians, 'Assess yourselves to check that you are living in the faith. Test yourselves to make sure' (13:5a, own translation). Or, in the words of the Psalms, 'Examine me, O God, and search me; test my heart and mind' (Psalm 26:2, own translation).

Lent is a time for a spiritual health check, an opportunity to look honestly at our discipleship and to ask if all is well. None of us is perfect, of course, and the last thing God wants is to encourage a spirit of negative self-criticism. Rather, he wants us to conduct an honest self-appraisal, and then to seek his gracious help in bringing inner healing and renewal. The cure does not lie in us any more than self-help remedies are the answer to every physical ailment. It lies in recognising something is wrong and seeking help from the one who alone is able to give us wholeness. If we are willing to admit our need, he will do the rest.

Chicken pox

Flu

Mumps

Toothache

Measles

Scarlet fever

PALM SUNDAY

The Servant King

Readings   2 Samuel 23:1-7; John 18:33-37; John 19:12-16

Aim   To contrast the kingship of Christ and the nature of his kingdom with that of earthly kings and rulers.

Preparation   No special preparation is needed for this talk.

Talk   Ask how many people are good at history. Most people will probably shake their heads, though a few may well be enthusiastic. Explain that you're about to find out, for you have prepared a quiz about various kings, queens and rulers, most, but not all of them, rulers of England. Ask if anyone can identify them from the following clues.

1
Became known as defender of the faith
Led the English Church away from Rome
Had six wives
Henry VIII

2
Some say he never actually lived
He had a sword called Excalibur
He is associated with a round table
Arthur

3
The last of the Saxon kings
He was defeated at the battle of Hastings
An arrow in his eye reputedly killed him
King Harold (Godwin)

4
She was a warrior queen
She ruled over the Iceni tribe
She was finally defeated by the Romans
Boudicca or *Boadicea*

5

He was king of Wessex
He was known as 'The Great'
He reputedly burnt the cakes
Alfred (the Great)

6

He originally came from Holland
He married Mary
He sounds like he ruled over a fruit
William III (of Orange)

7

He was also king of Denmark and Norway
He went on a pilgrimage to Rome in 1027
He tried to turn back the sea
Canute

8

He was ruler of England and Scotland during
    the Great Plague
He married Catherine of Braganza
He became king after the restoration of the
    monarchy
Charles II

9

He succeeded George V
He married Wallis Simpson
He abdicated shortly after taking the throne
Edward VIII

10

Walter Raleigh was one of her favourites
She was the last of the Tudors
She was queen of England at the time of the
    Spanish Armada
Elizabeth I

11

He went away on several crusades
He left his brother in charge of the country
He was known as 'The Lionheart'
Richard I

12

She ruled Britain longer than any other monarch
  [at the time of writing]
The British Empire was established during her
  reign
She has an era named after her
Victoria

13

He was known for his personal piety and love of
  justice
He was king of England during the Battle of
  Agincourt
A Shakespearean play is named after him
Henry V

14

She was the daughter of George VI
She has the same name as one of our greatest
  queens
This is the . . . year of her reign *(enter correct figure)*
Elizabeth II

15

He was the second Stuart King of England and
  Scotland
The Civil War started during his reign
He was eventually beheaded
Charles I

16

He was king of England from 978 to 1016
Danish raiders took him into exile
It sounds from his nickname that he was caught
  on the hop
Ethelred the Unready

17

He ruled an ancient civilisation
He was known as 'the Great'
His father, also king of Egypt, had the same name
Ramases II

18

He was eventually forced to commit suicide

He was blamed for the Great Fire of Rome

He was one of the instigators of the persecution of Christians

Nero

19

He was eventually poisoned

He suffered from various physical disabilities and a speech impediment

As emperor of Rome, he annexed Britain to the Roman Empire

Claudius

20

He was the first king of Israel

He suffered from fits of madness

He tried to kill David

Saul

21

He is attributed with writing the book of Proverbs

He was famed for his wisdom

He oversaw the building of the temple in Jerusalem

Solomon

22

He was appointed king by the Romans

His father had ordered all children in and around Bethlehem under the age of 2 to be killed

He was 'ruler' of Israel when Jesus was brought to him for trial

Herod

23

He rode into Jerusalem on a donkey

He was crucified as King of the Jews

He is still worshipped today by Christians as the King of kings and Lord of lords

Jesus

All of these kings, queens and rulers have one thing in common, except the last: they ruled over an earthly kingdom. They did so in different ways, with varying degrees of authority and in very contrasting styles. Some are remembered for their goodness, some are notorious for the mistakes they made or for the sheer evilness of their behaviour, but all would have enjoyed the trappings of state, the power and the prestige that comes with authority; all, that is, except one, once again.

The odd one out, of course, is Jesus. He came as king, but his kingdom was not of this world. He came to be crowned, but with a crown of thorns. He came not to serve himself but to serve others. That is the king we honour today: the King of love and Lord of life; the one who offered his life, who gave his all, so that we might share for ever in the joy of his kingdom.

An Eternal Kingdom

Readings Isaiah 9:6-7; Luke 19:36-38; John 18:33-37; 1 Timothy 6:13-16 (all to be read prior to the talk)

Aim This is another talk that makes use of history, but it takes a slightly different tack to the last, contrasting the transience of earthly kingdoms to the eternal kingdom and kingship of Christ.

Preparation In large bold letters, print the following, and arrange them in a column on a whiteboard:

1837-1901

1066-1154

1365-612 BC

1485-1603

500-336 BC

1652-1660

27 BC-AD 476

1550-1070 BC

1558-1603

1154-1422

967

1936-1938

1833-1837

613-616

Also print the following:

Isaiah

Luke

John

1 Timothy

Finally, you will need a marker pen to insert a colon in the final four 'dates' of the list.

Talk　Tell the congregation that, since it's Palm Sunday, the day on which we remember Jesus entering Jerusalem to be greeted by many as king, you want to think about rulers, kingdoms and empires, and that to help you do this you have prepared some important historical dates for them to consider. Ask if anyone can match the dynasty, empire or era to the appropriate date. The answers are given in italics.

You will need to explain that the Greek and Egyptian empires lasted for thousands of years, with various interruptions and invasions, but that the dates you have chosen are widely recognised as representing the pinnacle of those civilisations. You may also wish, prior to the talk, to print the answers and stick them alongside the relevant dates as each answer is given, even maybe displaying them on the board or around the church beforehand as clues.

1837–1901	*Victorian*
1066–1154	*Normans*
1365–612 BC	*Assyrian empire*
1485–1603	*Tudors*
500–336 BC	*Greek empire (Classical Age)*
1652–1660	*Oliver Cromwell and the Commonwealth*
27 BC–AD 476	*Roman empire*
1550–1070 BC	*Egyptian empire (New Kingdom)*
1558–1603	*Elizabethan*
1154–1485	*Plantagenets (including Lancastrians and Yorkists)*

Each of these represent eras in history where individuals or a succession of people from one dynasty have ruled over a nation or empire, yet all of them, even those dynasties that endured for thousands of years, are consigned to history. So what do you make of the remaining four dates in our list? (Point to the final 'dates' on the whiteboard. General puzzlement should ensue.)

Give the clue that these are not dates at all. Ask if anyone has any idea what they might be, and indicate that they have already been given a clue in the service. Place the slips of card / paper on which you printed the four names of books of the Bible in front of the four 'dates' and insert colons, as follows:

Isaiah 9:6-7

Luke 19:36-38

John 18:33-18:37

1 Timothy 6:13-6:16

The last four entries are in fact Bible verses, but each tells us about a ruler and kingdom unlike any of these. First, there's the prophet Isaiah (9:6-7):

> For a child has been born for us, a son given to us; authority rests upon his shoulders; and he is named Wonderful Counsellor, Mighty God, Everlasting Father, Prince of Peace. His authority shall grow continually, and there shall be endless peace for the throne of David and his kingdom. He will establish and uphold it with justice and with righteousness from this time onwards and for evermore. The zeal of the Lord of hosts will do this.

Then there's Luke, and one sentence used particularly of Jesus as he rode into Jerusalem on Palm Sunday (19:38a):

> Blessed is the king who comes in the name of the Lord.

Next there's the Gospel of John, and Jesus' words in chapter 18, verse 36, concerning the nature of his kingship and kingdom:

> My kingdom is not from this world. If my kingdom were from this world, my followers would be fighting to keep me from being handed over to the Jews. But as it is, my kingdom is not from here.

Finally, there's the first letter of Timothy, and one statement from that reading says it all (6:14b, 15b):

> . . . our Lord Jesus Christ . . . is the blessed and only Sovereign, the King of kings and Lord of lords.

All the other rulers and kingdoms we have considered lasted for a limited span only, each of them now merely dates in history, but with the kingdom of Christ it is different. He came to Jerusalem not to take up an earthly throne but to be raised up on a cross, his kingdom not of this world but beyond death. It is a kingdom many fail to see but one that is inexorably growing among us, each day moving us closer to that time when he will rule for evermore, here on earth as it is in heaven. So we worship him as King of kings and Lord of lords; the one who alone offers an eternal kingdom.

HOLY WEEK

An Amazing Price

Readings Matthew 10:27-31; John 3:16-21

Aim To emphasise that God was willing to pay the ultimate price to overcome everything that keeps us from him.

Preparation Print the following in large bold letters, and display on a whiteboard:

GOLF CLUB	£50	£106,000	£500,000
PLAYING CARDS	£21	£2,555	£99,000
COW	£914,000	£1,245,000	£5,000,100
PIANO	£1,999,999	£1,450,000	£2,300,100
TOY	£2,324	£39,050	£128,333
MEAL	£298.02	£13,091.20	£18,176.07
NUMBER PLATE	£2,000,000	£9,000,000	£15,000,000
PEN	£169,000	£749,000	£1,000,000
HOUSE	£18,000,200	£31,367,400	£62,767,500
WATCH	£8,500	£91,247	£6,820,450
BOTTLE OF WINE	£982	£2,001	£2,435
CHEQUE	$634	$1,667,500	$9,000,000,000

Talk Begin the talk by holding a light-hearted auction for charity (auction something simple, like a homemade cake, hand-knitted scarf or such-like). See how high the congregation are willing to go in their bidding.

Afterwards, explain that you are going to play an unusual version of the TV show *The Price is Right*. Each of the items in question was sold for what was then a world record, but can anyone guess the price? Run through the list of items on your display board, displaying the name of the item and the three prices on the board. Below is the correct price, together with additional information.

- GOLF CLUB: A Scottish putter was sold for £106,000 and is now on display at Valderrama Golf Club in Spain
- PLAYING CARDS: A pack of playing cards was sold to the Metropolitan Museum of Art in New York for £99,000
- COW: A Friesian cow was bought at auction in Vermont for £914,000
- PIANO: A Steinway piano once belonging to John Lennon was bought by George Michael for £1,450,000
- TOY: An antique toy hosepipe was sold at auction in New York for £128,333
- Meal: A meal for three at Le Gavroche in London cost £13,091.20
- CAR NUMBER PLATE: In 1994 a car number plate was sold in Hong Kong for £9,000,000
- PEN: A pen made in Switzerland and called 'La Modernista Diamonds' was sold in London for £169,000
- HOUSE: In 1997 a house was sold in Hong Kong for £62,767,500
- WATCH: A watch was sold at auction in New York for £6,820,450
- BOTTLE OF WINE: A bottle of 1993 Beaujolais Nouveau was sold at auction in the same year for £982
- CHEQUE: The largest cheque ever written was by Mitsubishi, to Morgan Stanley, in autumn 2008

In all of the above we are talking about astonishing amounts of money, a price that some people were willing to pay but that most of us wouldn't even dream of. Yet even the highest figure that we can think of is as nothing compared to the price that God was willing to pay to redeem us; a price that is spelt out in the Gospel of John (3:16, own translation): 'God loved the world so deeply that he gave his only Son, so that anyone who believes in him will not die but will enjoy everlasting life.' Why did he do this? Because we are good, deserving, worthy? No, the answer is in the words of Jesus recorded in Matthew (10:29-31, own translation): 'Are not a couple of sparrows sold for one pence? Yet not even a single bird will fall to the ground without your Father noticing. Believe me, he has numbered even the hairs of your head. Don't be frightened, then; you are more precious than many sparrows.' That's why God was willing to pay the ultimate price, ready to offer his own Son for the life of the world: because each one of us is of infinite value to him, unique and precious, someone to be treasured. Unworthy we may be; in his eyes we are nonetheless of limitless worth.

The figures we have talked of today, and the items they were spent on, are truly astonishing, but the fact that God was willing to give so much for those as undeserving as us is more astonishing and more marvellous still!

Meekness and Majesty

Reading Mark 15:16-39

Aim To illustrate how in the death of Christ on the cross we glimpse both his meekness and majesty.

Preparation Print the following in large bold letters:

> BLOOD, CROWN, THORNS, CROSS, NAILS, HANDS, FEET, THIEVES, FORGIVE, DIE, SPEAR, SON OF GOD, LOVE, GRACE, MEEKNESS, MAJESTY

Cut out each letter and attach magnetic tape to the back, and then arrange on a board as follows:

S	L	O	V	E	M	C	R	O	S	S
O	F	D	I	E	E	F	E	E	T	T
N	O	M	A	J	E	S	T	Y	T	H
O	R	H	C	N	K	S	B	G	H	I
F	G	A	R	A	N	P	L	R	O	E
G	I	N	O	I	E	E	O	A	R	V
O	V	D	W	L	S	A	O	C	N	E
D	E	S	N	S	S	R	D	E	S	S

Talk Explain that you want to think about the meaning of the cross, and, in particular, about the words used in the Graham Kendrick hymn, 'Meekness and majesty'. Ask if anyone can answer the following questions, each of which is found somewhere on the display board. As each correct answer is given, remove the letters from the grid and rearrange them at the bottom of the board.

1. What did Jesus say he would shed as he shared wine at the Last Supper? (his BLOOD)

2. What did the soldiers place on to Jesus' head? (CROWN of THORNS)

3. What was Jesus made to carry before being crucified on it? (CROSS)

4. What did the soldiers hammer into Jesus? (NAILS)

5. Where did they hammer them? (HANDS and FEET)

6. Who were crucified either side of Jesus? (THIEVES)

7. What did Jesus ask God to do to his enemies? (FORGIVE)

8. What did Jesus do after he cried out 'It is finished'? (DIE)

9. What did the soldiers thrust into his side to make sure that Jesus was dead? (SPEAR)

10. Who did the centurion at the foot of the cross say Jesus was? (SON OF GOD)

11. What did Jesus say we can show no greater example of than in laying down our life for our friends? (LOVE)

12. What 'amazing' thing do we see in the fact that Jesus died for us? (GRACE)

Your display board should now look like this:

```
                    M
                    E
        M  A  J  E  S  T  Y
                    K
                    N
                    E
                    S
                    S
```

BLOOD CROWN THORNS CROSS NAILS HANDS FEET THIEVES FORGIVE DIE SPEAR SON GOD LOVE GRACE

The two words left are, of course, MEEKNESS and MAJESTY, and it is no accident that we can arrange those in the form of a cross, for both of them are seen so powerfully in the death of Jesus. On the one hand, we see there the one who accepted a crown of thorns rather than an earthly kingdom, the one who was crucified alongside thieves, allowing nails to be driven into his hands and feet, the one who was ready to die for us, shedding his blood as the spear was thrust into his side. For those, though, with eyes to see, here was the Son of God, the King of love, and the most wonderful example of the grace of God. Here was God and man, suffering servant and crucified Saviour, the one who died so that we might live. Meekness and majesty: two sides of the one Lord, revealed so graphically in the cross.

Changing Faces

Reading Various Bible verses are included as part of this talk.

Aim To explore the changing emotions underlying Holy Week (from Palm Sunday through to Easter Day), and to illustrate that God is with us even in times of confusion, sorrow, despair and fear, able to restore faith, joy, hope and trust.

Preparation In large bold letters, print the following verses and stick them on a whiteboard or in conspicuous positions around the church.

> Jesus said, 'Now my soul is troubled.' *(John 12:27)*
>
> They . . . fled from the tomb, for terror and amazement had seized them. *(Mark 16:8)*
>
> The whole multitude of the disciples began to praise God joyfully. *(Luke 19:37)*
>
> His disciples did not understand these things at first. *(John 12:16)*
>
> He denied Jesus again, angrily. *(Matthew 26:72)*
>
> He found the disciples asleep, weary through sorrow. *(Luke 22:45)*
>
> Jesus said, 'Do not let your hearts be troubled, and do not let them be afraid.' *(John 14:27b)*

On separate pieces of paper, print the following: Confused, Sad, Amazed, Troubled, Overjoyed, Angry, Afraid. Fold up the pieces of paper ready to distribute among volunteers during the talk.

Talk Ask the congregation how good they are at pulling faces. Invite seven of the young people to come forward to have a go. Hand out the words on the pieces of paper you prepared prior to the talk, one per volunteer. Ask each volunteer to pull a face expressing the named emotion and then take a poll of the congregation each time to see whether they can guess what face is being pulled. Ask each time if someone can spot a verse matching the expression (the matching pairs are given below).

> Jesus said, 'Now my soul is troubled.' (John 12:27) – Troubled
>
> They . . . fled from the tomb, for terror and amazement had seized them. (Mark 16:8) – *Amazed*
>
> The whole multitude of the disciples began to praise God joyfully. (Luke 19:37) – *Overjoyed*
>
> His disciples did not understand these things at first. (John 12:16) – *Confused*
>
> He denied Jesus again, angrily. (Matthew 26:72) – *Angry*
>
> He found the disciples asleep, weary through sorrow. (Luke 22:45) – *Sad*
>
> Jesus said, 'Do not let your hearts be troubled, and do not let them be afraid' (John 14:27b) – *Afraid*

Our mood and feelings can change just as easily as our faces, as Holy Week so powerfully reminds us. One moment, as Jesus rode into Jerusalem, the crowd were overjoyed, celebrating and praising God, welcoming him as God's promised Messiah; the next, they were angrily shouting 'Crucify!' 'We have no king but Caesar!' One moment, the disciples were professing undying loyalty; the next they had scattered to save their skin, Peter angrily denying he had ever known Jesus. One moment they were looking to the future full of hope; the next, they saw cause only for fear; joy, faith and confidence giving way to sorrow, fear and confusion. Even Jesus himself experienced the trauma of emotional turmoil in the Garden of Gethsemane as he faced up to the prospect of death.

Yet the emotions of Good Friday were to be transformed once again in the days that followed, as the risen Christ appeared first to Mary and then to his disciples. Doubt and confusion were replaced by faith, sorrow by joy, despair by hope and fear by confidence. They realised that even in their darkest hour, God had been there, identifying with them and working out his purpose.

There is the truth at the heart of Holy Week: that the suffering, evil and darkness which had seemed victorious was not some ghastly mistake but woven into God's purpose, death paving the way to new life for all. Whatever we may experience, remember that ours is a God always at work and able to transform each and every situation, however hopeless it may seem.

EASTER

The Difference Easter Makes

Readings   John 20:1-29; Galatians 1:13, 22-23

Aim   To emphasise the transforming power of God's love, supremely shown in the resurrection of Christ.

Preparation   Copy, enlarge and cut out the following pictures of the tomb of Jesus, and print on the back of each in large bold letters DOUBT and FAITH respectively. (Larger versions of these pictures may be found on page 75.)

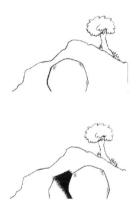

Using pieces of sturdy card, cut out four large long thin rectangles, two vertical and two horizontal, the latter slightly smaller than the others. In as large letters as possible, write out the following words on the back of the rectangles, as follows:

J O Y L O V E V I C T O R Y	E N D D E A T H H A T R E D

DESPAIR   SORROW   DEFEAT

HOPE   BEGINNING   LIFE

Next, copy and enlarge the two pictures below and stick these on to two separate boards.

Finally, using small pieces of sticky tack, stick on the rectangles (arranged into the shape of a cross, words facing downwards), and the tomb shapes, to make two separate 'tableaux', one a 'scene' of Calvary and the other of the empty tomb. (NB. The Calvary scene uses the 'End, Death, Hatred' and 'Despair, Sorrow, Defeat' cross pieces, and the empty tomb scene uses the 'Joy, Love, Victory' and 'Hope, Beginning, Life' cross pieces.)

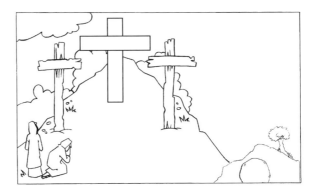

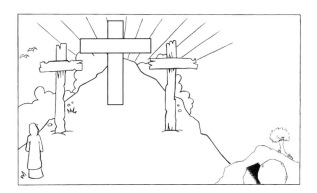

Larger versions of the pictures may be found on pages 76-77.

Talk Display the two pictures you have prepared and tell the congregation that one represents Good Friday and the other Easter Day. Ask if anyone can spot the differences between them (eight in all: extra figure in first picture, no sunshine in first picture, extra cloud in first picture, extra birds in second picture, grass missing in second picture, stones missing in second picture, different markings on left-hand cross in second picture and of course the stone rolled away from tomb in second picture).

There are eight differences that we can see almost immediately, though of course the only differences we are actually told of are that it was dark on Good Friday with the stone rolled against the tomb, but light on Easter Day and with the stone rolled away. There are, though, other important differences between Good Friday and Easter. Let me show you what those are. (Turn over the central cross and the tomb in each picture and then stick these back in position so that the words are showing.)

After the death of Jesus, the cross must have symbolised all the things in the first picture: a place where hatred had triumphed over love, despair over hope, sorrow over joy, death over life; a place of defeat where all his followers' dreams had come to an end, faith in consequence giving way to doubt. But on Easter Day all that changed, for they came to realise that Jesus was risen and alive, the cross not what they had imagined after all but used by God in the fulfilment of his purpose. Far from the way things had seemed, love had triumphed over hatred, hope over despair, joy over sorrow, life over death; the cross had become a place of victory – and all at once faith was reborn.

That's what we celebrate today: the glorious message of the empty tomb and the wonderful truth that in the suffering and agony of the cross God was supremely at work.

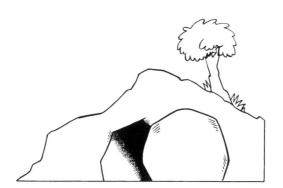

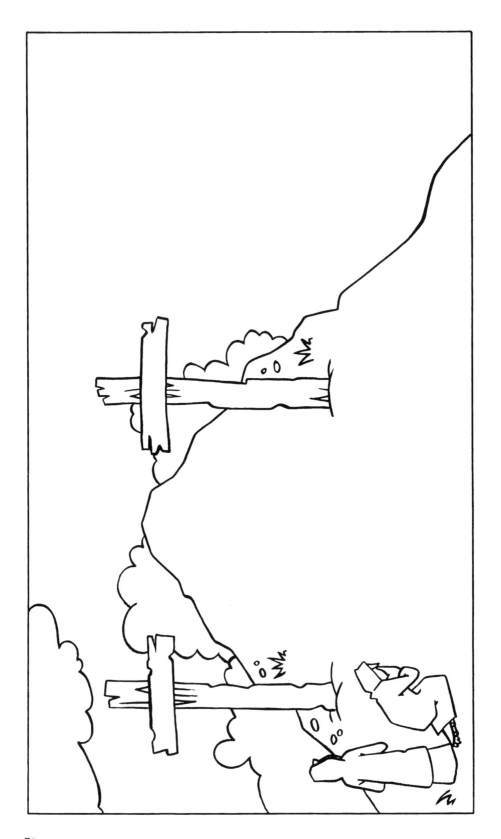

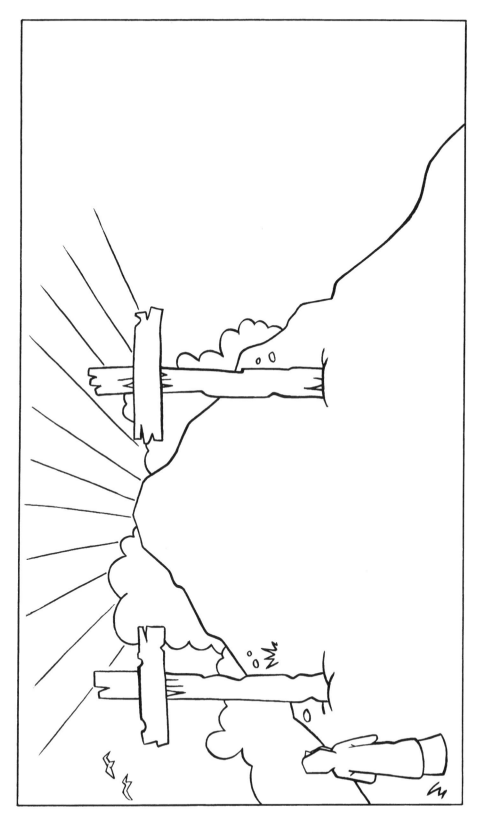

Easter Transformation

Reading John 20:1-29

Aim This talk, like the last, focuses on the way Easter turns around not just death but every aspect of life.

Preparation On separate squares of thin card, one per letter, print the following:

> TROUBLE
>
> HOPELESS
>
> FRIGHTENED
>
> CONFUSED
>
> UPSET
>
> AFRAID
>
> SCARRED
>
> DISPIRITED
>
> STUNNED
>
> ALL ALONE
>
> BEATEN

Attach small pieces of magnetic tape or sticky tack to the back of each letter, and keep the set of letters for each word separate, ready for use later in the talk.

Talk Tell the congregation that you want to compare the feelings of the Apostles and followers of Jesus in the time immediately after his death and then following his resurrection. To do so, you have two 'quizzes' for them: the first concerned with the former feelings and the second concerned with the latter. Read out the following clues, inviting people to guess the answer (offer prompts, if necessary) and as each correct (or more-or-less correct) answer is given, arrange the letters (one by one) on a whiteboard, to spell the word out (arrange these words in a column down the left side of the board):

- Something we get into as children when we're naughty *TROUBLE*
- The word describing a situation where there seems to be no future *HOPELESS*
- Another word for scared *FRIGHTENED*
- Another word for puzzled *CONFUSED*
- May mean we're sad or in tears, or that something's been spilt *UPSET*
- Another word for scared and frightened *AFRAID*
- We are this when we have a mark left by a physical or emotional injury *SCARRED*
- A word meaning having lost heart or lost enthusiasm *DISPIRITED*
- We may be left feeling this by a physical or emotional blow *STUNNED*
- Two words meaning that we're totally abandoned *ALL ALONE*
- A word meaning that we've lost a contest or been thrashed by someone *BEATEN*

All of those words describe how the followers of Jesus felt in the days following the death and burial of Jesus. They were *frightened*, *upset* and *confused*, *stunned* by what they had seen and left feeling *all alone* in a hostile world. They believed Jesus and everything he stood for had been *beaten*, and they were *afraid* of what *trouble* they might face as a result. Understandably, they felt *scarred*, *hopeless* and *dispirited* by their experience, all their dreams having apparently been crushed.

But all of this is to reckon without the miracle of Easter and the glorious message of resurrection; a resurrection that was to extend into every aspect of their lives. To help illustrate the transformation Easter brought, consider the following clues. (As each correct answer is given this time, remove the letters you need from the words on display, and make a fresh column of new words on the right-hand side of the board. At the end, all the letters should have been reused.)

- Jesus told Nicodemus that we need to be this if we would be Christians *REBORN*
- This means being sure of yourself or without any doubts *CONFIDENT*
- Another word for happy or overjoyed *DELIGHTED*
- A word meaning confident, guaranteed or in no doubt *ASSURED*
- Another word for sure *CERTAIN*
- A word meaning enthused or brilliant *INSPIRED*
- Another word for brave, daring or courageous *FEARLESS*
- This means promising or optimistic *HOPEFUL*
- Another word for amazed or astonished *ASTOUNDED*
- A word meaning positive, optimistic or looking on the bright side *UPBEAT*
- Two words meaning prepared or ready to go *ALL SET*

The words we had before have totally gone, having given way to words with a completely different meaning. As they discovered the empty tomb and then met with the risen Lord, the followers of Jesus were *delighted* and *astounded*, suddenly *hopeful, upbeat* and *confident* about the future. Faith was *reborn*, so that they felt *certain* he would be with them, *assured* of his guidance whatever they might face. The days that followed were to see those who had been frightened and hesitant turned into *fearless* and *inspired* disciples, *all set* to do whatever was asked of them.

The transformation could hardly have been more complete, and it is a transformation that God goes on making in all those who respond to Christ, resurrection taking place each moment of every day in their lives. The message of Easter is not just about the disciples or others, but also about what God has done for us.

Faith Restored

Reading   Luke 24:13-35

Aim   To bring home the fact that resurrection involves not only life after death but renewal in every area of life.

Preparation   In very large letters, print the word FAITH and stick it to a piece of thick card. Cut the card into a simple jigsaw of 15-20 pieces. Affix segments of magnetic tape to the back of each puzzle piece (if you do not have a magnetic board, use sticky tack when it comes to reassembling the broken jigsaw later in the talk), then make up the jigsaw on a large non-magnetic board and lay this on a table in the church.

Talk   Tell the congregation that you have been busy making a jigsaw that you very much want to show them. Pick up the board as if to hold the puzzle up and clumsily allow the puzzle to slip off and crash to the floor, where, hopefully, the pieces will come apart (if they don't, then separate them as you stoop down to pick the puzzle up). Express consternation, and ask for help in putting the puzzle back together again. Enlist the help of a couple of volunteers, and rebuild the puzzle to reveal the word FAITH.

The jigsaw puzzle, of course, is a simple one, but the word it reveals, and the way we've rebuilt it, carries an important message, for, just as the puzzle was broken into pieces, so too was the faith of the Apostles as they witnessed the agony and death of Jesus on the cross. They had followed him for three years, slowly coming to recognise him as the Messiah, and they had expected, somehow or other, for Jesus to ride into Jerusalem and establish God's kingdom, but instead they had seen him arrested, mocked, flogged and tortured. For all of them it had been a crushing blow, and as Jesus was laid in the tomb so their hopes and faith were buried with him.

That's what we see in the two disciples walking home along the Emmaus Road. 'We had hoped that he was the one to redeem Israel,' they say of Jesus to the stranger who suddenly joins them. Such hopes, though, had been cruelly crushed as they watched Jesus die on the cross, and now, even though they have heard from the women who went to anoint his body that the tomb is empty they refuse to believe it. Their faith lies in pieces, like their shattered dreams. Until, that is, they stop and break bread with this man who has joined them, and afterwards light dawns, hope returns, faith is reborn as they realise that he was none other than Jesus, alive as the women had said, risen just as he had promised before his death.

At that moment, they too came alive again, life transformed, the future full of promise and the present given new meaning. They knew then, as they would know for the rest of their lives, that resurrection not only gave them hope of life to come but new life then and there, restored and reborn every day. That is the truth of Easter that we in turn celebrate today. Thanks be to God!

Telling the News

Reading   Matthew 28:1-20

Aim   To emphasise that the good news of Easter is something we are called to share.

Preparation   Record on videotape brief excerpts of television newsreaders (about 15 excerpts, if possible). Set up a television and video in the church that can be clearly seen by all, and ensure that the video is rewound to the beginning of the first excerpt. Double-check everything is working smoothly to make sure you are not caught short in the talk. (If organising a television facility is difficult, this talk could be successfully given using an audio recording only.)

Talk   Play the video clips, asking the congregation to identify each newsreader. These are all people whose job it is to read the news. We rely on them to tell us what's going on, to keep us informed, to make sure that we're aware of anything important happening around us.

Though we may not have the makings of a newsreader, there's a sense in which we're all called to do the same, as the words of our reading make clear: 'Go, then,' says Jesus, 'and make disciples of all people, baptising them in the name of the Father, the Son and the Holy Spirit.'

Do people recognise us as those who have something important to share, as those who tell the news?

ASCENSION

A Different Dimension

Readings   Luke 24:50-53

Aim   To show that the Ascension was the final catalyst in helping the Apostles to grasp the true nature of Jesus, it fully revealing his glory.

Preparation   Using large letters on a whiteboard or OHP, print the following:

A B ... D E

$101 + 11 = \ldots$

$MCL =$

40 pence x 6 = . . .
MICE

Talk   Tell the congregation that you have some absurdly simple questions that you want their help in answering. Ask the following, one by one, pointing to the whiteboard where appropriate, and express astonishment each time someone gives you the 'correct' answer, pronouncing it incorrect instead. Build up the congregation's mood of puzzlement as you go through, appearing to become increasingly incredulous at the wrong answers suggested.

- What's missing from the following? A B ... D E?
  (Refer to white-board)
  The natural but 'incorrect' answer is 'C'.

- What is the answer to the following? $101 + 11$
  (Refer to whiteboard)
  The natural but 'incorrect' answer is 112.

- What does MCL mean? *(Refer to whiteboard)*
  The natural but 'incorrect' answer is 1150.

- What year is it?
  The natural but 'incorrect' answer is the year in which you are giving this talk.

- What is the capital of this country?
  The natural but 'incorrect' answer is 'London'.

- How many books are there in the Bible?
  The natural but 'incorrect' answer is 66.
- What time is it?
  The natural but 'incorrect' answer is the exact time you ask the question.
- How much is the following? *(Refer to whiteboard)*
  The natural but 'incorrect' answer is £2.40.
- What fuel do most cars use?
  The natural but 'incorrect' answer is 'petrol'.
- Where would you find Birmingham?
  The natural but 'incorrect' answer is in the Midlands of the UK.
- What is Elizabeth Taylor famous for?
  The natural but 'incorrect' answer is 'for being a film actress'.
- How many yards are there in a mile?
  The natural but 'incorrect' answer is 1760.
- What does the word 'piano' mean?
  The natural but 'incorrect' answer is 'a musical instrument'.
- Where would you find Washington?
  The natural but 'incorrect' answer is 'in the USA'.
- What are MICE? (Refer to whiteboard)
  The natural but 'incorrect' answer is 'small rodents'.

At the end of the 'quiz', ask who's feeling confused. Then, go through the questions again, this time giving the following 'correct' answers.

- What's missing from A B … D E?
  G (gamma) if following the Greek alphabet.
- What is the answer to 101 + 11 = …?
  8 if using binary numbers.
- What does MCL mean?
  It's an abbreviation meaning Master of Civil Law.
- What year is it?
  According to the Jewish calendar, it's 3762 years later than the current year according to the Gregorian calendar.

- What is the capital of this country?
  In Roman times, the capital was Colchester.

- How many books are there in the Bible?
  The Roman Catholic Bible has 73 books.

- What time is it?
  In Sydney, Australia, the time is 14 hours earlier than here (i.e. add ten hours to find the correct time).

- How much is 40 pence x 6
  In pre-decimalised money it makes £1.

- What fuel do most cars use?
  According to the Americans, most cars run on gas (or gasoline)!

- Where would you find Birmingham?
  There's a place called Birmingham in Alabama in the USA.

- What is Elizabeth Taylor famous for?
  Elizabeth Taylor (1912-1974) was a British novelist born in Reading.

- How many yards are there in a mile?
  There are 2025 yards in a nautical mile.

- What does the word 'piano' mean?
  The word piano in a musical score means 'softly'.

- Where would you find Washington?
  There's a place called Washington in northeast England.

- What are MICE?
  MICE are engineers; that is to say, Member of the Institution of Civil Engineers.

You can see that all the answers you gave, just like all those I've given you, are both right and wrong. Birmingham is in the Midlands, there are 1760 yards in a mile, 101 + 11 *does* equal 112, MICE are rodents, C is the third letter of the alphabet, and so on. Each of the questions can be looked at in two different ways, and the answer we give depends on how we approach it.

The same is true of so much of life. There is often more to something than meets the eye, as the disciples slowly came to learn was the case with

Jesus. At the beginning of his ministry, when he first called them to follow him, they probably saw him as little more than a gifted teacher and preacher; someone special, certainly, but not, as they later came to see him, the Son of God. Even when Peter made his celebrated confession of faith in Jesus as the Messiah, what he meant by the term was very different to what Jesus meant. When Jesus rode into Jerusalem on Palm Sunday, his followers still expected him to claim political authority and an earthly kingdom. So when they saw him instead nailed to a cross it must have seemed that everything they had believed was wrong, a terrible and tragic mistake. Even after he rose again they didn't fully grasp who he was and what it meant. Their faith was constantly growing as they looked behind Jesus' humanity to his divinity, as they glimpsed God behind the man. And in the mysterious event of Ascension, in whatever it was that happened on that day, they came to realise as never before that he was both one with them yet one with God. He was a king, but his kingdom was not of this world. He came to bring new life, but life of a different quality and dimension. He had died, but death was not the end. The cross, which had seemed a place of defeat, was in fact the place of victory!

On the day of Ascension, the disciples finally realised that they had been giving the wrong answer because they had failed to understand the question; they had looked for one meaning when Jesus had been pointing to another.

What of us? Have we glimpsed the full wonder of what God has done for us in Christ? Do we recognise his living presence with us now? Are we awake to the signs of his kingdom all around? Ascension reminds us that Jesus is greater than we can ever begin to imagine; that he offers a new dimension to life, a different perspective to each day, and a fuller experience of God's sovereign power, awesome love and unfailing grace.

A Glimpse of Glory

Readings Mark 16:1-14; Acts 1:6-11; John 1:14

Aim To emphasise that just as the disciples only gradually came to grasp the full glory of Jesus, so our understanding of who he is and what he has done should be constantly growing.

Preparation On a piece of card (ideally, of good thickness and several feet across), write out the word GLORY, using as large letters as space permits. Cut out these letters, so that you have letter-shaped holes in the card. Cover these holes over from behind with pieces of coloured tracing paper or crepe paper (for added effect, use overlapping pieces to cover each letter, thus creating a mosaic/stained-glass window appearance). Next, cover over the front of the letters with thick pieces of card, three pieces to each letter, fitted together so that they do not overlap. Use sticky tack for this so that each piece can be easily removed as questions are answered during the service. The pieces of card need to have the following initials written on them, one initial/set of initials on each:

P
B
C
S
P
N E
L J G
N A
J B B
R
M
T
N A
H C
P, J and J

When you have finished preparing this display, position it in a prominent position at the front of the church, preferably at eye level, and set up two or three desk lamps behind it to create a back-lighter effect shining through the letters once the pieces of card covering them are removed.

Talk   Tell the congregation that you have something very special to show them at the front of the church but that to see it they need first to answer some questions. Pointing to the appropriate initial/s, ask the following questions, removing the appropriate initialled card once a right answer is given and thus slowly revealing the word GLORY underneath:

1. Which bird beginning with P gives a glorious display by raising its tail feathers? *Peacock*

2. Which B begins as a humble caterpillar but emerges in a glorious new form from a chrysalis? *Butterfly*

3. Which C exchanged her rags to go to the ball in glorious style until midnight? *Cinderella*

4. Which small white flower beginning with S gives a glorious display for a few weeks early each year? *Snowdrop*

5. Which bird of ancient mythology beginning with P was said to rise gloriously from its ashes? *Phoenix*

6. Which part of America, beginning N E, is celebrated for its glorious autumn colours? *New England*

7. Which L J G enjoyed the glory of being Queen of England for nine fleeting days? *Lady Jane Grey*

8. In which N A do we find the words 'happy and glorious, long to reign over us'? *National Anthem*

9. Which song, with the initials J B B, has a chorus that begins, 'Glory, glory, hallelujah'? *John Brown's body*

10. Which great empire, beginning with R, reached as far into Britain as Hadrian's Wall but now leaves only a few traces of its former glory? *Roman*

11. Which M came down off Mount Sinai with his face radiating the glory of God? *Moses*

12. Which glorious ship, beginning with T, sank on its maiden voyage? *Titanic*

13. Which N A experienced his moment of glory as the first person to walk on the moon? *Neil Armstrong*

14. What glorious sight can be seen in the sky every 76 years? *Halley's Comet*

15. Who glimpsed the glory of Jesus at his so-called transfiguration? *Peter, James and John*

Ask the congregation what word has been revealed. The answer, of course, is GLORY, and the more questions we asked, so the more glory shone through until it could be fully seen. But what sort of glory are we talking about? Our questions were concerned with brief moments of glory associated with certain individuals, creatures, plants or objects, but such glory is a short-lived thing, here today and gone tomorrow.

Our readings point to a different sort of glory: the glory of Christ.

It was glimpsed first by Peter, James and John in the mysterious event known as the transfiguration. High up on a mountaintop they came to recognise Jesus as the fulfilment of the law and the prophets, the promised Messiah, reflecting God's glory as Moses had done on Mount Sinai centuries before. Yet if this was a glimpse of glory, the full picture was only to emerge later, as, following his death and resurrection, Jesus was taken from their sight and they realised as never before that he was not just sent by God but was one with him, sharing his glory. So John writes in his Gospel (1:14):

And the Word became flesh and lived among us, and we have seen his glory, the glory as of a father's only son, full of grace and truth.

Was this the end of story? No, it was only the beginning, for it meant that there was always more to understand; the full wonder of Christ, as with the wonder of God, being something that we can never exhaust. As Christians we should constantly be uncovering new insights into his glory, seeing a little more fully the wonder of his grace and truth, for however much we may have glimpsed, there is always more to be revealed.

PENTECOST

People of the Spirit

Reading   Galatians 5:13-26

Aim   To highlight what should be essential characteristics of 'people of the Spirit'.

Preparation   Draw two large ovals and display these on separate whiteboards. Underneath one write CHRIS and under the other write IAN.

Next draw and cut out the following shapes (you will need to ensure they are to scale with other features of the face that you are going to create with them):

- Four ovals, to serve as eyes
- Two mouth shapes
- Four ear shapes
- Two irregular shapes, to serve as noses
- Two large crescent shapes to serve as hair
- Four smaller crescent shapes to serve as eyebrows

Try to make the two sets of features distinctive. Print, in as large letters as possible, the following on the back of these shapes:

Ears	Self-control / Patience (one on each)
Nose	Kindness
Hair	Generosity
Eyes	Love / Peace (one on each)
Mouths	Gentleness
Eyebrows	Faithfulness / Joy (one on each)

Stick the shapes with a small piece of sticky tack in conspicuous places around the church, with the words facing downwards.

Talk   Tell the congregation that you need to draw up a photo-fit of a couple of people you've been hearing about called Chris and Ian. Ask people to look around the church and see if they can spot the parts of a face that you need to build up each picture. Ask in turn for a mouth, eye, nose, etc. until both faces are complete.

Tell people to have a good look at these and ask if anyone has seen them. Then announce that you've just realised that this is a case of mistaken identity, the character you're looking for being one person, or rather the name given to a certain kind of person and people. Ask if anyone can spot what the name is. The answer, of course, is Christian, the letter 'T' missing in between CHRIS and IAN.

So what does a Christian look like? To answer that we need only look around this or any other church. In other words, Christians come in all shapes and sizes, there being nothing physically different or distinctive about any of us. The difference is not on the outside, but the inside, so let's consider what we might find there. Turn over the various components of the faces, and read out what is on the back of each piece, either once again arranging these in the shape of a head, or simply displaying them at random. Love, joy, peace, patience, kindness, generosity, gentleness, faithfulness, self-control – these are the things that God wants to see in our lives, the sort of qualities that should characterise a Christian. The Bible calls them fruits of the Spirit, for these are not qualities we can acquire through our own efforts alone, coming rather through being open to God's Spirit and ready to let that Spirit work within us. Yet if God plays his part we must also play ours, looking to grow in faith, to respond to the Spirit's guidance and to cultivate our relationship with Christ. None of us recognised the photo-fit pictures we put together, because of course they weren't real people. The question is, will anyone recognise us as Christians, or will they see us too as a sham?

Experiencing the Unseen

Readings   John 3:1-15; 1 Corinthians 12:1-12

Aim   To bring home the fact that though we cannot see the Holy Spirit, we can experience the Spirit's power in our lives and see evidence of it in the lives of other Christians.

Preparation   For this talk, all you need is a small portable radio, though make sure that the volume can be turned up loud enough for it to be heard throughout the church. You will need to have preset stations, or to know which frequencies various stations are tuned to.

Talk   Ask how many people listen to the radio, which station they like best, which programme they most like listening to, and who is their favourite DJ or presenter. Tell the congregation that you are going to give them a radio test. Tune one by one to the following stations, asking if people can guess which station each one is: Radio 2, Radio 4, local radio station, Classic FM, Radio 1, Radio 5, foreign radio station (as a catch question), Radio 3, Virgin Radio, World Service. Take several answers, and perhaps a poll of the congregation each time, to ensure maximum participation among all those present.

All of those radio stations and programmes are being broadcast all over the country – in the case of the World Service, all over the world. The air is full of radio waves, not to mention TV signals, yet, of course, we cannot see any them, or hear them without a radio to receive them. We know they are there through experience, having simply to turn our radio on to prove it, but they themselves are hidden from human sight. So it is also with the Holy Spirit. As Jesus told Nicodemus, when speaking of being born again, 'The wind blows where it chooses, and you hear the sound of it, but you do not know where it comes from or where it goes. So it is with everyone who is born of the Spirit' (John 3:8). We cannot pin down how the Holy Spirit works or through whom he works. We cannot physically prove to others that the Spirit is anything other than our imagination. But when we turn to Christ and commit ourselves to him, we experience the presence of the Spirit within us: the peace, power, guidance and inspiration that only the Spirit can give. And if the Spirit is indeed at work, then that will show in the way we live and the gifts we show, in whether the fruits of the Spirit are in evidence and our gifts used in his service.

As the Apostle Paul reminds us, '[w]e look not at what can be seen but at what cannot be seen; for what can be seen is temporary, but what cannot be seen is eternal (2 Corinthians 4:18). Though we cannot see the Spirit, never underestimate what he is able to do in our lives.

Fruit, Not Flowers

Readings   1 Corinthians 14:1-19; Galatians 5:16-26

Aim   To emphasise that the presence of the Holy Spirit is shown not by showy gifts but by living fruits.

Preparation   On separate strips of paper / card, print the following in large bold letters:

MARIGOLD, LUPINS, ANTIRRHINUM, GERANIUM, CHRYSANTHEMUM, ROSE, FUSCHIA, ASTER, DELPHINIUM, SWEET PEA, TOFFEE, MELBA, MERINGUE PIE, AND CREAM, AND CUSTARD, WINE, JUICE, SPLIT, FRITTERS, SORBET, ROLLS, PINEAPPLE, RHUBARB, LEMON, BANANA, PEACH, STRAWBERRIES, ORANGE, APPLE, MELON, FIG, ELDERBERRY

Attach magnetic tape or sticky tack to the back of each, and arrange on a board as follows:

MARIGOLD MERINGUE PIE

LUPINS AND CREAM

TOFFEE FUSCHIA

GERANIUM AND CUSTARD

ROSE MELBA

SWEET PEA WINE

ANTIRRHINUM JUICE

CHRYSANTHEMUM FRITTERS

ASTER SORBET

DELPHINIUM ROLLS

HOLLYHOCK SPLIT

Retain the remaining words for use later in the talk.

Talk   Ask the congregation how much they fancy the mouth-watering delicacies you have spelled out on the board. Express mock surprise at their disinterest, and ask what's wrong with the dishes – in other words, what they ought to read. As people come up with the answers, remove the wrong word and insert the correct one, as follows:

LEMON MERINGUE PIE

STRAWBERRIES AND CREAM

TOFFEE APPLE

RHUBARB AND CUSTARD

PEACH MELBA

ELDERBERRY WINE

ORANGE JUICE

PINEAPPLE FRITTERS

MELON SORBET

FIG ROLLS

BANANA SPLIT

There's nothing wrong, of course, with flowers – indeed, the world would be a sadder and less beautiful place without them – but we don't generally want to eat them. Fruit is a different matter. It *can* look attractive and even be grown for ornamental purposes, but we usually grow it for food, for the express purpose of eating. In some cases, flowers may be a stage on the way to fruit, but in terms of usefulness it's the fruit we're after.

Perhaps this is why Paul referred to various God-given qualities as 'fruits of the Spirit' – things like love, joy, peace, patience, kindness, generosity, faithfulness, gentleness and self-control. Not only can these qualities be seen but they also affect the way we live and the people we are. They are not simply there for show, but are a visible harvest of the Holy Spirit's presence within us.

So it is that Paul, writing to the Corinthians, warns of the danger of coveting showy spiritual gifts. Of course, gifts of the Spirit have their place, but only insofar as they are complemented by spiritual fruits, and, above all, by love. Pentecost reminds us of the day when power came upon the Apostles, enabling them to preach to a multitude in a variety of tongues, but we should never forget that it reminds us also of the way countless lives both then and across the centuries have been changed through the fruits of the Spirit being nurtured within them. How far do such fruits testify to the work of the Spirit within you?

TRINITY

Beyond Comparison?

Readings Isaiah 40:18-26; 46:5-7; 2 Corinthians 13:13

Aim To emphasise the truth that the only way we can do justice to the wonder of God is through recognising him as Father, Son and Holy Spirit.

Preparation No special preparation is needed for this talk.

Talk Ask the congregation if they can define what a simile is (i.e. a word that compares one thing to another, using the word 'like' or 'as'). Ask if anyone can supply the missing word from each of the following well-known similes:

As common as ?	*muck*
As bald as a ?	*coot*
As tough as ?	*nails (or old boots)*
As meek as a ?	*lamb*
As bold as ?	*brass*
As ugly as ?	*sin*
As cool as a ?	*cucumber*
As fit as a ?	*flea (or fiddle)*
As daft as a ?	*brush*
As flat as a ?	*pancake*
As light as a ?	*feather*
As warm as ?	*toast*
As good as ?	*gold*
As mad as a ?	*hatter (or March hare)*
As pleased as ?	*Punch*
As pretty as a ?	*picture*
As clear as a ?	*bell (or as mud or as crystal)*
As red as a ?	*beetroot*
As safe as ?	*houses*
As snug as a ?	*bug in a rug*
As dull as ?	*ditchwater*

As straight as an ?	*arrow*
As keen as ?	*mustard*
As stubborn as a ?	*mule*
As white as a ?	*sheet*
As busy as a ?	*bee*
As clean as a ?	*whistle*

When it comes to God, comparisons are not just difficult but impossible, for every metaphor or simile we may use can, at best, point to a fraction of the truth, each concealing as much as it reveals. However many words we may pile up to speak of his power, love, grace or goodness, they will always be inadequate, for he is infinitely greater than all of them put together. As the prophet Isaiah puts it, 'To whom, then, will you liken God, or with what likeness will you compare him? An idol? It is cast by a workman and a goldsmith gilds it and casts silver chains for it. The one unable to afford this selects wood that will not rot and seeks out a craftsman to create an idol that will not topple over' (Isaiah 40:18-20, own translation). Or as the Psalmist asks, 'Who on high can compare to the Lord? Who among the heavenly host is like the Lord, a God revered in the assembly of the holy ones, great and awesome above all those around him?' (Psalm 89:5-7, own translation).

So does this mean that God is beyond comparison? Almost, but not quite, for though no words or image can hope to express his greatness, three terms give us some kind of picture of who he is: the terms 'Father', 'Son' and 'Holy Spirit'. The first reminds us that God is the giver of life but at the same time likens him to a father; one, in other words, who loves and cares for all his children. The second reminds us that God in Christ has shared our humanity, walking our earth and experiencing both life and death, and thus revealing God's nature and purpose through word and deed. The last reminds us that though we do not see him we experience God's presence within us, at work in our lives and in the world, nothing able to contain or limit him.

Trinity Sunday reminds us that we need to keep a sense of God's greatness that is beyond comparison, yet to recognise also the way we experience that God as Father, Son and Holy Spirit. So, along with the Apostle Paul, we not only can say with our lips but can also mean in our hearts: 'The grace of our Lord Jesus Christ, the love of God, and the companionship of the Holy Spirit, be with us all' (2 Corinthians 13:13, own translation).

A Sense of Proportion

Reading   Ephesians 3:16-21

Aim   To stress the importance of Trinity Sunday in reminding us of the overwhelming scale of God's greatness.

Preparation   Print the following riddle on a large piece of card/paper, in large, bold letters.

> My first is in MEGA as well as in GREAT,
>
> My second's in WOW but not UNDERSTATE,
>
> My third is in WONDER and found in ADORE.
>
> My whole calls forth worship expressing our awe.

Print the riddle again in microscopic letters on a tiny piece of paper.

Talk   Tell the congregation that you have a simple riddle for them to solve. Stick the tiny version on to a whiteboard, and ask who can solve it. Of course, no one will be able to because no one will be able to read it! Ask what the problem is, and then display the larger version. This time, the congregation should have no problem in solving the riddle to reveal the word GOD.

Often in life we need to get the bigger picture before we can understand what's going on, and the same is true when it comes to God. Our picture of him is often far too small, disproportionate to the reality. To illustrate what I mean, take a look at the following picture:

Ask what's wrong with the first picture, and allow people to identify all the features that are out of proportion. Afterwards, display the 'corrected' picture, as follows:

(Larger versions of these pictures may be found on pages 113-114.)

When drawing, we need to ensure that we keep things in their proper proportion, and the same is true when it comes to thinking about God, as we see in our reading today. Paul grasps at every proportion imaginable to express the wonder of God's love in Christ. 'I pray,' he writes, 'that Christ may so dwell in your hearts through faith that you will be able to grasp with all the saints the breadth, length, height and depth of the love of Christ; and that you may know this all-surpassing love in such a way that you will be filled with the very fullness of God!' (Ephesians 3:14a, 17-19, own translation). This love, says Paul, is beyond measure, bigger than anything we can ever begin to comprehend and reaching out in any and every direction, nothing and nowhere being outside of its scope. And if that's true of God's love, it's all the more true when it comes to describing or defining God himself. However great we may believe he is, he is always greater still, on a scale that leaves us gasping in amazement. The only way we can begin to express that wonder is through the three labels, God the Father, God the Son and God the Holy Spirit. Why? Because those three persons point to his presence above, beside and within us, different dimensions of one reality. Overemphasise a single aspect at the cost of the others and our picture of

God becomes distorted and unbalanced. We need a sense of God's majesty and splendour, an awareness of his constant companionship and friendship, and an experience of his power and presence deep within. All are part of the picture but none are the whole.

Don't let your picture of God be too small or out of proportion. Learn the message of Trinity and glimpse a little more clearly the breadth, length, height and depth of who God is and what he means.